LAUGHING AT LIFE

ED KAISER

Kathleen,
I hope laughing will
keep you young at heart
forever

Ed Kaiser
2015

ISBN 978-0-9891462-4-1
Printed in the USA

Published by Buttonwood Press, LLC
P.O. Box 716, Haslett, Michigan 48840
www.buttonwoodpress.com

I dedicate this book to my wife, Sue.
Without her encouraging laughter,
my antics and skewed perspective
would have never become written words.

ACKNOWLEDGEMENTS:

I believe this is the space allocated to the author for thanking those who've been particularly helpful in producing this book. Without question, my wife, Sue, is at the top of the list. Not only does her laughter motivate me to write, she is also the primary inspiration for much of what I write about. She's the leading lady of my life as well as the star of many of the stories in this book.

Other significant people in the process of putting my foolishness in understandable print are Anne Ordiway, Editor, and Joyce Wagner, Proof Reader. Note, I said understandable. Often my mind works either neglectfully faster or time-lapse slower than my fingers depress the appropriate keys. Additionally, my word processor's intuitive edits do not always agree with my intentions. The resultant text has more lint than a sheep barn. Somehow, Anne and Joyce sort through all that fluff to salvage the yarn from the fuzz.

But wait. After all the phrasing is improved, spelling corrected and comma's strategically placed, the electronic bytes of my humorous bits must be transformed to digital images, ink and paper. As a writer, I pay little attention to such things as margins, centering, script or glyphs. I think a glyph might be a glitch corrected, but I'm not sure. Sarah Thomas surely knows though and her typesetting skills provide, pleasing to read, digital images. The ink and paper are supplied by Color House Graphics, Grand Rapids, MI under the watchful eye of

Sandy Gould. Hmmm, now that I say this, I'm wondering what her other eye might be doing.

Except for the possibility that I somehow coerced you to buy this book, something made it attractive to you. For that visual attraction, I am certainly grateful to Dawn Baumer. Without her delightful artwork catching your eye, it is quite possible this copy would still be gathering dust on a bookseller's shelf.

There is one more person to thank, and it goes without saying.

What? You were expecting me to actually state what goes without saying?

Though I'm uncertain as to how something which is not said, actually goes anywhere, I suppose I should at least hint to the obvious that goes without saying. Do publishers have issues?

Yup... that's the hint. Hinting aside, I will be forever grateful for Richard Baldwin's confidence to issue this book as well as his insightful publishing expertise.

It is quite a task for all of these folks to process my whimsical thoughts into the book you are holding. Without each of them skillfully accomplishing their part of the enterprise, my "Friday Frivolities" would remain archived text files. "Friday Frivolity" is the title I have used for years in reporting my weekly perspective of happenings around me. I chose that heading for two obvious reasons—Friday was the day of distribution and Frivolity was an alert that the content was definitively joking about whatever life had offered me that week. It was also considered as the title of this book. It was not chosen for the obvious—you are not restricted to reading it on Friday, or it might lead you to believe that Fridays are my only days of merriment.

That is certainly not the case. Each day, I easily find amusement in what many folks might consider as mundane. Mundane is just reality without aberration. Admittedly, it's quite possible that my mind, itself, is an aberration... or, at least, an anomaly of normal thought processing. However, I believe if you release the constraints on your imagination, most events of life have pleasurable potential. I hope these instances I share from my life will inspire you to discover amusement in commonplace experiences.

A NOTE FROM THE AUTHOR:

My **Question of the Day** is typically rhetorical. Generally, there is no correct answer. In fact, most of them are hardly worth any consideration beyond the chuckle it hopefully generates.

Often some event, sighting, or spoken phrase launches a punny pin ball in my skull, which bounces wildly about my brain seeking a rational resting place. If logical reasoning fails to quell the mental commotion, the **Question** escapes through my keyboard to potentially disturb the sanity of friends.

With each story, I will share a **Question of the Day.** Though you may try to deduce a sensible response, I believe your most enjoyable moments would come from playing with words in similar context or contemplating a witty come back. After all, **Isn't a good pun its own reword?**

QUESTION OF THE DAY:

Is the jam we need help getting out of, made from the pickle we got into?

I believe it is noteworthy that most jams we find ourselves trying to get out of, result from our own doing… or more likely, undoing. After all, if I had not gifted my wife, Sue, the dollhouse, there would have been no pickle for me to get into.

1

Dollhouse

Did I mention that I got my wife a dollhouse for Christmas? BIG mistake! I had no idea what I was getting into. Why didn't someone warn me? Assembling bikes for your kids may be a nightmare, but building a dollhouse with your wife is comparable to events in a Steven Spielberg horror story.

What? You think it's just a matter of nailing floor A to walls B, C and D, then slapping a roof over it all? Oh, no—you've got to *finish* the floors first. Geez, I've got Armstrong NO WAX flooring in my bathroom for a reason. I don't do floors. And my idea of gluing some terrycloth down and calling it carpet wasn't taken very seriously.

So, it's off to Home Depot. Gel stain, shellac and shellac thinner—we only needed a couple ounces of each but those particular products don't come in containers that small.

"Sure… we'll take a half pint," I say. "Oh, I see, quart is the smallest." And to make matters worse, we weren't even going to use it full strength.

Oh well, even though I haven't used shellac since Cub Scouts, I'm sure we'll find some use for it.

As it turned out, I spilled some while stirring, so I went ahead and shellacked my whole work bench.

Anyway, back to our Home Depot shopping trip...

"And while we're at it, dear, we might just as well get paint for the outside walls and stain for the shingles," said my excited wife.

"Shingles... you're not suggesting we're gonna stain 10,000 quarter-inch-square shingles?"

"Don't be silly! ...There's less than a thousand, I'm sure."

Oh, that's a relief. Now my fingers will be a much lighter shade of blue-green.

But finishing floors, papering walls, and staining shingles are not the worst part of this continuing saga.

"Guess what, Ed?" was Sue's leading question as she read the assembly instructions.

Now, I've learned that "Guess what...?" is not really a question. It's very similar to "Ya know what I've been thinking?" and should always be considered as a warning.

It makes absolutely no difference how I respond. Even if I say "I don't want to know!" I'm still going to get an astounding tidbit of information that will most likely stupefy me. So, I quietly slink back to the nearest wall like a man standing in front of a firing squad and say, "What, dear?"

Sue continued. "It says here; if you are going to electrify your house," (Click—I hear a gun's hammer being cocked.)

"...you must first install the wiring." (Was that a muzzle flash?)

"Well, yaaah... I'm going to have lights in the house!" (Ouch, the first bullet hits me.)

"Come on, let's go get the wiring." (Not now, dear. Can't you see I'm bleeding?)

"Look at this, Ed, it doesn't look like it will be hard to do." (I feel my strength slowly ebbing away.)

"This will be fun, won't it, hon?" (Call the morgue; I'm a goner.)

"Electrify the house?!?" I retorted, "with my luck, I'll electrify *myself*."

Then I almost said, "Do I look like an electrician?" but thought better of it, considering, at that moment, I looked more like a pallid corpse than anything else.

So the fun began. Off to Hobby Hub for wiring.

Now, I'm not so foolish to believe I could just use some left over #10 wire I've got in the basement, but I certainly didn't have any idea that the wiring could get so tiny and yet have such a huge price-tag.

The wiring kit had everything: Twelve-volt transformer (at least I won't get electrocuted), wire (actually self-adhesive copper tape), brass nails (must be they've seen me use self-adhesive tape before), miniature outlet-sleeves, and a nail/sleeve guide (essential to protect my fat fingers while trying to pound on practically-invisible nails). And all for the everyday low price of... oh, well, so much for the $75 gift certificate I included with the dollhouse kit.

There I was, looking for a bag to stop my hyperventilating when Sue comes up with a little blister pack. "Look at these cute little switches."

"Switches? You're not suggesting I try to install wall switches!"

"Sure. They're the exact scale of the house."

Why, I've seen *fish* scales that were bigger. "I am not installing any miniature switches!"

"How will I turn on the lights without switches?"

"It's call a plug. ON... you plug in the transformer. You want the lights out, unplug it. Elementary, my dear. By the way, are there really elements in those lamps?"

If I put those tiny switches in her dollhouse, she'll have to buy a miniature finger to turn them on and off.

A few days passed, and we have now managed to assemble the floors to the walls and Sue has done the floor-finishing. Done, that is, except for waxing and buffing. I suppose now she'll want to buy a miniature buffing machine.

QUESTION OF THE DAY:

When I give someone a piece of my mind, why doesn't it fit in theirs?

I have given others far too many pieces of my mind. Though I'll admit that there have been times when the piece I'm giving is in rebuttal, most often I offer it to enhance the moment, not degrade it. Many such opportunities come while talking on the phone.

2

It's For You

Sometimes Sue doesn't pay attention to caller ID. Sometimes the 'system' doesn't really know how to ID the caller. I'm not sure which was the case when Sue handed me the phone one evening. "It's for you."

I pushed the speaker-phone option. "Hello."

There was no response, so I repeated my greeting a bit louder. A male voice then began... "I'm calling to tell you about an opportunity..." The voice was not familiar, yet I easily recognized the tone, or monotone as was the case. At first, I thought it was a recording and my mind shifted into high "Survey Stumper" gear.

A distinct voice inflection when he mentioned a name changed my impression. It was not a recording, but a real human. Though I had not recognized the person he was calling on behalf of, the name which did register was Ellie's Restaurant. It's a quaint, locally-owned and -operated place in downtown Williamston.

He continued reading his script, which included something to the effect of: "...*he'll be discussing what's happening at the Capitol.*"

Immediately my mind downshifted, or more precisely, downgraded, into "Who Cares?" gear. Let's face it, if I distrust the organization, why would I grant credibility to one of its agents?

When the caller inquired, "Does this sound like something you would be interested in attending?" my voice took on the persona of a 90-year-old. Not that there is anything necessarily disparaging about being 90, but I think there is better chance for humor in the simplistic logic of that stage of life. I enjoy it so much that I have every intention to achieve that age.

My simplistic reply: "Is it free?"

"Free? Well... yes... there is no charge to attend."

"No, I mean is breakfast free?"

"I'm sorry, sir. I don't believe he will be paying for breakfast."

"Bummer."

"I'm sorry... what did you say?"

"I guess your hearing isn't any better than mine. What I said was, 'Bummer.'"

"Yes, I guess you could say that."

"Not what I *could* say. That's exactly what I did say. It's a bummer that he won't buy my breakfast."

"I'll, ah... I'll make a note of that. I'm sure... he..." I could tell he was having a difficult time talking between snickers, so I interrupted.

"I mean, if I'm gonna come listen to him, the least he could do is buy my breakfast."

"I'll be sure to let him know."

"You do that. I like breakfast, and Ellie has good ones. Maybe he'll buy next time."

"Then I assume that you are not interested in coming this time."

"Not if he ain't buyin'. Fact is, if he ain't gonna buy next time, you don't need to bother to call me then, either. I don't very often go out unless someone else's buyin'."

He could hardly hold back his laughter as he closed; "I'll make a note of that also. Good bye."

Gee, I hope he didn't mean he was going to take me off of his calling list. Such calls are very entertaining for me. Sue, too. She was laughing heartily in the other room. She was also wondering why she had handed me the phone in the first place.

"Well," I reminded her, "You said, 'It's for you'." But, in a way, I hope the call ended up being for the other guy, too.

QUESTION OF THE DAY:

Is it a disorder to be out of sorts?

I have some chronic disorders. If I don't see my physician or a specialist sometime during the month, I have withdrawal pangs… which is immediate cause for an appointment. I'm not saying I'm a hypochondriac. It's just that I don't avoid medical investigations as they certainly can be therapeutic.

3

Life's a Gas

Last week, a long-time friend of mine was lamenting about *growin' old* because her maladies were mounting a considerable assault on her well-being. Hmmm, my maladies are giving me wonderful opportunities for entertainment and edification. Each time I see a specialist or go in for some procedure, I marvel at the amazing things modern medicine has to offer.

The other day I had an Esophogram. What an incredible experience. I mean to tell you, this equipment was a lot bigger than Star Trek's tricorder, but almost as impressive as it peered into my body. I got a chance to see the monitor briefly as the doctor scanned my swallowing technique. Yikes! It looked like a python swallowing one white mouse after the other.

Of course, that thought did have a somewhat detrimental effect. When it hit me that each gulp I was making coincided with another white mouse heading for my stomach, I had a slight involuntary, convulsive ripple in my stomach. But, hey, they've got people to clean up the little puddle that escaped onto the table.

What did they expect, anyway? Laying a guy down on his stomach and asking him to imbibe plaster of Paris through a straw is just asking for puddles. I hope they didn't let that stuff dry too long. Late in the afternoon, I was still chiseling remnants of that concoction from my mustache.

But that wasn't the only stuff I had to drink. When I first arrived in the examination room, the attendant nurse advised me of what was to come.

"I'm going to mix these crystals in this water and you will need to drink it as quickly as possible."

"No problem," I replied.

"I mean you must drink it *immediately* and *completely*. These will act like Alka-Seltzer and put a considerable amount of gas in your stomach and esophagus. You'll feel like belching, but please refrain."

"Wait just a minute. Hold on there. You're going to deprive me of a primal pleasure of Male-dom? Are you tellin' me, you're gonna fill my belly with gas, and I can't burp?"

"That's correct. We need that gas to remain there to expand the stomach and esophagus to enable a clear picture."

"Well, here's a little different picture. You've starved me for 18 hours to shrink my stomach. Now you're going to induce bloating. Why didn't you let me eat a juicy breakfast at my favorite diner? I could have burped and there'd still be plenty of expansion in there for a clear picture."

She laughed, but otherwise ignored my plight. "Then we'll ask you to slowly, but steadily, swallow the contents of this cup."

She handed me a large cup containing several pounds of nearly-congealed concrete.

"Are you kidding? I don't need to actually *swallow* this. My dear, if you pour this into my mouth it WILL go down... swallow or not."

Again, a chuckle, but no compassion. "I'm going to raise this table to the upright position and then you can just step up onto the platform, and we can begin."

Wow, was that slick. They raised the transporter table to vertical. I fully expected to see "Bones" McCoy enter the air lock any minute.

Anyway, up on the platform: Lights off, camera on, down with the Alka-Seltzer, and I quickly started sucking on the straw of the other liquid. Have you ever tried drinking plaster through a straw? What's worse is trying to down that triple-thick potion with a belly full of Pop Rocks effervescing more CO_2 than a case of champagne. Abstinence from belching was the least of my worries.

But, you know what? That stuff didn't taste bad at all. I'm not good at flavors. It wasn't exactly piña colada, but kinda fruity. More like a banana shake. Hmmm, I think my mind imagined that flavor because it felt like whole bananas slithering down my throat. But at least the flavoring helped suppress the gag reflex.

All in all, it was a rather exciting morning. I got a chance to witness some amazing technology, had delightful interactions with some fine people, and came away with a full stomach… and no aftertaste.

So you see, the maladies associated with growing old aren't really so bad, providing you have the proper perspective. Life's a gas.

At least that morning it was.

QUESTION OF THE DAY:

Do the bonds of matrimony lose value when interest goes down?

I assure you the interest in our bonds has gone up every year of our marriage. Every day we reinvest in each other. The payoff is frequently realized in...

4

An Adventure With Sue

I didn't write last week because Sue and I were on an adventure. 'Twas a road trip to Oklahoma and back. More specifically, to Fort Sill, for Chelsea's graduation from Army Basic Training. Of course, we combined that occasion with visits to historical sites… some of it along nostalgic Route 66… and scenic wanderings.

The trouble with making such a journey in January is limited sunlight. During summer months, Sue and I plan to see things long into the evening. In the winter, after 5, headlights are about all that's visible. I mean… seriously? It doesn't take long to point out all the subtle color variances of headlights.

Whether we were using darkness to travel across great expanses of Oklahoma's parched pastureland or checking into a hotel early because all the exciting sites close at dusk, Sue wanted something to occupy her mind. So, she took her laptop computer.

Actually, occupying Sue's mind is more a necessity than luxury. Her Attention Deficit Blessing (we try to keep a positive perspective) almost requires her to multitask. At one point on our trip, Sue was playing solitaire on her laptop and sipping a chocolate shake while talking on her cell phone. I looked over, and I think she was actually swaying with the music on the radio too. It's often astounding to me in how many tasks Sue can simultaneously, and effectively, engage.

Well, effectively so long as conversation is not one of the tasks, but conversation was not particularly required as we sang along with sentimental tunes on the radio. We also use Garmin. No, on second thought, we depend on that monotonous feminine voice to guide us to destinations. On the open road, I can manage to sing, glance at Garmin, and keep the car between the lines.

However, when Garmin interrupts the Beatles with "*In seven tenths of a mile...*", I need Sue's undivided attention. Unfortunately, "undivided" is a virtual impossibility for Sue.

Not only does the radio music mingle adversely with Ms. Garmin's droning, her computerized representations of "*right*" and "*left*" are not always discernible in my computerized interpreters... better known as hearing aids. Therefore, I need Sue as a human interpreter.

I was quite certain Garmin's instruction was to "*Exit Right*". Even in the darkness, a left exit was clearly downhill, and downhill is exactly the direction Sue's conversation took. "Ed, you need to exit right then turn... there's the hotel over there, we're staying at the... and look, over there's a place we can... oh, wow, that's one of my favorite songs from the 60s."

Now you see why our trips are so adventurous.

QUESTION OF THE DAY:

Can your karma
run over your dogma?

Most of nature intrigues me. I could sit and watch animal activity for hours on end. However, there is one aspect of nature which brings out my worst karma.

5

Despicable

I despise squirrels. Actually, I despise what squirrels do to me. So, I guess it's a toss-up as to who is more despicable.

The other day, I scrambled out the front door angrily chasing one of those miserable rodents across the yard. Dogs chase squirrels, though they never catch them. Dogs are dumb. Yet there *I* was chasing one. I threw a snowball in its general vicinity and hollered "…and don't come back!"

Yeah, right. Even if it understood English, my threat was hardly intimidating. I'm just slightly faster than a slug pulling an anvil and I'm only 50% successful at hitting a large tree with a snowball. So there I stood. Mission aborted. Snow melting into my slippers.

Why? What could possibly cause my sanity to disintegrate so quickly?

The squirrel had been eating from my bird feeder. I put those seeds out to attract birds, not rodents. If the squirrel's there, no birds. If the squirrel eats all the sunflower seeds, most of my favorite birds don't come. I don't want squirrels at my feeder.

I tried squirting pepper spray on the seeds. The squirrels said, "Ole'."

I gave them food at a site some distance from the bird feeder. They called in their buddies, devoured the distracting bait, and came to the feeder for dessert.

I set out a cage-trap with a savory mound of peanut butter and nuts. They ignored it. At least they ignored it until the latches froze open. Then they safely gobbled down the tantalizing treat.

Incidentally, our bird feeder is a brightly-colored, grotesque iron sculpture of a rooster. Its creator told us the squirrels would not come near such a menacing creature. I love the rooster, but it fails shamefully as a deterrent.

The other morning, I spotted one of the glorified rats sitting on the back of the rooster. I threw open the front door and charged out. He scampered off. I had barely gotten back inside when he returned.

Again, I launched out the door. In a flash, he zipped around the corner of the house. It was hardly a minute before he returned. A third time I clambered out the door. This time he jumped from the feeder, stopped, and turned to see if I would give chase. I flailed my arms and headed for him. Gone. I started to go back inside and glanced at the corner of the house. He reappeared. He just sat there, forefeet crossed in a prayerful pose, awaiting my next move. I stepped inside and let the storm door close. Immediately I reopened it and peered toward the corner of the house. That miserable scoundrel was scurrying toward the feeder.

That was the last straw. I'd had it with his persistence. He'd pay for this. I began to formulate a plot to shoot him. I don't own anything more powerful than a BB pistol, but that would at least sting for a day or two. A fourth time I caused him to scamper around the corner, then I headed for the garage rather than return to the house.

In the garage, I quickly loaded my BB pistol and crouched in ambush. His path from the corner of the house to the feeder was clearly within my sight. I waited in the shadows, squinting down the gun-sight through a crack in the doorway. A minute went by. The ice cold pistol drained heat from my fingers. Another minute... two... several... and still no squirrel in sight.

Now, sub-freezing temperatures initiate shivers. Another minute went by with still no fuzzy rat in sight. The wind gusts through the cracked-open door made my eyes water. The gun sight blurred, but I waited motionless—except for the spasms now shaking the pistol. Still I waited, wondering why I hadn't put on long-johns, or at least a coat, before embarking on this frigid hunt. Finally, with numbness creeping from the garage floor into my toes, I decided my fingers were too stiff to pull the trigger. I called the hunt off and went back into the house.

I shall not tell you how long it was before the squirrel returned. I can tell you, however, it was shorter than the thaw time for my nose. After my brain defrosted, I got this sickening thought: What if that despicable rodent *had* returned? What if I *had been* able to squeeze the trigger? What if my teary eyes and convulsing arms *had* spoiled my aim just a tad? What if the BB *had* ricocheted off the wings of my repulsive rooster into our picture window?

I wonder—can a man commit suicide with a BB pistol?

QUESTION OF THE DAY:

Why is it that so many people want to feed your pet peeve?

My father frequently cautioned me to choose my words carefully lest they be misunderstood. In practice, I actually think he chose his phrasing for potential mitigation when put on the spot for what he purportedly said. I wouldn't exactly call it a pet peeve, yet when something I've stated is misconstrued, I… well… let's just say, I feel a little blue.

6

Blueberries

"I love blueberries!"

That's my response now to any statement about me hating blueberries. Many moons ago I made an offhand comment that I preferred just about any other fruit to blueberries. Okay, so maybe I said, "I don't like blueberries." Somehow that statement was construed to mean I hate blueberries.

It's strange that Sue would misconstrue "don't like" to "hate". You see, she hates mushrooms. Oh, no, that's not an exaggeration. If a few happen to escape her scrutiny when scooping from a casserole containing mushrooms, she will quickly extricate them from the amalgamation on her plate lest they further contaminate her serving. That, ladies and gentlemen, is categorical *hate*. I do not separate blueberries when they happen to infiltrate my scoop of mixed fruits. Of course, I do not strive to gather an abundance of them in the scoop, either. I think you'd agree, I do not *hate* those acidic, teeth-staining, grizzly-skinned, not-even-close-to-bite-sized fruits.

Considering a recent discovery Sue has made, I might just have to change to actually *liking* blueberries. According to research she trusts, consuming a half-cup of blueberries each week significantly reduces the chances for dementia... or at least slows its invasion of the brain. Of course, when she advised me of this preventive alternative, my inquiring mind asked, "How do they affect the *advancement* of dementia?" She admitted she didn't have a clue.

As you might suspect, my mind cannot handle vacuums created by unanswered questions. I quickly formulated a somewhat logical possibility.

It's an acceptable maxim that the color blue has therapeutic value. It is considered to have a calming effect. Thus, I propose that the staining properties of blueberries somehow course through human veins. I imagine white blood cells... ah, yes, the healing corpuscles, bond with sub-atomic molecules of blue hue. When dementia attempts invasion of brain cells, the now pale blue blood cells release the stain—coloring, calming, and curing affected brain cells. No longer do the cells die— they dye. The effect is cumulative and irreversible. Grey matter is transformed to ever-deepening hues of blue.

That idea may be harder to swallow than the blueberries themselves. Sue wasn't exactly choking on my initial attempt to rationalize the consequential effect of blueberry intake in thwarting dementia, but she wasn't swallowing it either. Undeterred, I concocted a better theory for Sue to contemplate.

Considering that blue is the color of speed... What? You've never heard of a bolt from the blue; blue streak; blue blazes... ooops, wrong context. Don't wanna go there.

Anyway, it's a scientific fact the hottest portion of a flame is blue as well as the predominant color of high-intensity electrical sparking. Ah, yes, and electrical impulses are the means of neurological transmission of data in the brain. Well, then, I suppose that the blueberry staining of neurons could expedite clear brain waves. There you have it. That's it exactly. Blueberry-stained neurons enhance brain waves, thus forestalling dementia.

Pass the blueberries please. It's obvious my brain is in need of their therapeutic effects.

QUESTION OF THE DAY:

If we agreed on everything, wouldn't one of us be unnecessary?

Sue and I do not agree on everything, yet I certainly would not suggest we disagree either. It's simply that we have varying perspectives. Her viewpoints are as valid as mine. Our respective attitudes in regard to any given instance each have merit and lead us to equitable agreement. Neither of us are wrong. However, she is always right.

7

Closet Space

"**E**d, there's no room left in your closet," Sue exclaimed from our bedroom. "You've got so much clothing crammed in this closet, I can't get in another shirt. I'm going to move some stuff to another closet."

Hmm, I'm not sure why my wardrobe could possibly need a second closet. What's a guy need two closets for? Women do because they've got fabric texture, neck-line, hem-line, style-line and color lines—or the absence thereof—to consider when getting dressed. Sleeve length is about all I contemplate. Okay, maybe I consider shirt-color if I'm going to wear a suit. But for everyday wear, I just make a pot-luck grab into the zone of either short or long sleeves.

Another reason I can't imagine how my closet suddenly became overcrowded: I only received two new shirts for Christmas. So, even though Sue just finished the laundry, fitting in two more shirts shouldn't present much of a problem.

"You're kidding, right?" I said doubtfully from across the hall.

"No, I'm serious. I'm going to move your suits to the guest-room closet."

I accepted her need to move my suits. Nevertheless, I was still a bit suspicious of what I considered an exaggerated assessment.

As she went back into our bedroom, I made it clear that I didn't want her to presumptuously toss any of my shirts into the rummage.

"Seriously? Then why did you have this 'retro' shirt behind your suits?"

"It's a stage shirt. I've kept it just in case I need it for a costume."

"It's a costume, all right. Okay, I'll put it back. At least it's an XL. Now that you've lost weight, it probably will fit you." I'm sure glad she didn't calculate how many years that shirt has been waiting for me to get back to wearing XL.

However, she did calculate how many shirts I have. "Forty-three," she proclaimed. "You could wear a different shirt every day for two months."

See, I told you she was exaggerating. Two months would be 61—not 43.

Of course, 61 is also significant in another context. That's about the year in which I bought that shirt—and it was stylish, not "retro". In the fifty years since, styles have changed drastically, yet I still love that shirt even if it's now categorically *"retro"*.

And there are several others in my closet which fit that category, whether they fit my torso or not. In regard to my shirts, I believe nostalgia wins out over style. Hey, how can you tell if a man's shirt is from the 60s or current? Except maybe for distinctly *hippie* designs, I'll bet you can't tell micro-fiber from polyester in my closet. Even the shirt in question was more what Dobie Gillis would wear than Maynard G. Krebs. Come on, now. Button-down plaid will always be *far out cool* in my mind.

Another reason for the overabundance of shirts is my penchant for good rummage-sale buys. Because most of my yard-sale clothing was bought in the last few years, it is a bit large. Ah, but "too big" is good for my emotional well-being. When I wear the large shirts, I get lots of praise for the amount of weight I've apparently lost. Yo, any of you guys out there who've lost some weight but nobody has noticed, come on over! I've got some shirts that will give you TV's "Biggest Loser" look. Sue will verify that. Well, at least she has inferred that I've got some "big losers" in my closet.

QUESTION OF THE DAY:

Don't you wonder what cured ham was cured of?

I believe the word cure is derived from the Latin word for care, most applicable as medical attendance. Kind of makes you wonder how that fits with pedicure and manicure and there is no medicure. But insofar as what medi-cure could mean, there is definitely a lot of medical attendance needed to develop a cure.

8

Ultrasound Needed

What would you think if someone complained of frequent bouts with... well... like a cramping sensation accompanied by yucky feelings... you, know... like morning sickness? What would be your assessment if other symptoms were inexplicable—mood swings, depression now and then, and a belly big enough for twins?

Perhaps you would surmise a pregnancy. My doctor disagreed, primarily because I'd have been the first male to accomplish that miracle.

However, just as he would have done for a female patient with similar symptoms, he scheduled me for an ultra-sound—at the Women's Center no less. There should be a medical directive: No man should be required to go to a Women's Clinical Center. They are not equipped for such a venture.

First of all, when you go to most medical centers, there's a receptionist. How else would you know where to go? How else, if you're a guy, anyway? Women might instinctively know exactly what door to enter.

Men need people to talk to. Intuitive we're not. I only find a desk with a dozen signs but no human to talk to.

And not one of the signs said "Ultra-sound, this way".

"Over here, Ed," says my much more intuitive wife, "They're waiting for you in the Breast Care Center."

"Yeah, right... I'm sure they are," I replied a bit cynically. "Who's perverse idea was it to schedule a man for anything in the Breast Care Center?"

Inside, wall-to-wall women, all staring, wondering why a man was signing in. I was beginning to wonder myself. And so was the gal at the window. "What are you here for this morning, sir?"

"I'm auditioning for the Jerry Springer Show," I say brightly.

"Sir?"

"I have an appointment for an Ultra-sound."

"Fine, have a seat," she says, indicating one apart from all the ladies. I'd hardly gotten comfortable in my seat when a tech called me. That's the fastest I've ever been rushed out of a waiting room. What did they think? Either they've watched way too much Jerry Springer and figured I might be telling the truth, or I was going to get some perverse pleasure out of mingling with pending mammograms. Actually, I think the women were staring at me more than I was at them. At any rate, I was happy for their expedience.

I was quite excited at the opportunity to experience an Ultra-sound. I told Jennifer, the technician, that I'm always intrigued by medical technology, and this was my first pregnancy. She smiled and did her best to calm me… facetiously of course.

After a few formality questions (not surprisingly, geared toward women), I was on the table, and she was probing my belly with that jelly-smeared camera. I tried to see the screen. "You'll have to remain still, Mr. Kaiser."

"Well, then, can you turn the screen so I can see?"

"There's not much to see, sir."

"Will you take pictures for me to show my friends?"

"Pictures?"

"Yeah. My daughter got Ultra-sound pictures of her baby."

"But you're not pregnant."

"You can tell already? You've only been looking for a minute or two. Keep looking—maybe you can find an alien."

"I'm supposed to be looking at your gall bladder."

"Okay, but a gall bladder could be an exciting picture to some people. What else can you see in there? Breakfast? Do the raisins show up clearly?"

"Yes, as a matter of fact, I can see your breakfast… and quite a bit of gas, as well."

"Gas? You can see gas?"

"Actually, gas is an interference. But gas isn't as much interference as your trying to look at the screen. Lie *still*."

After she took a few shots up under my ribs, she asked me to roll on my right side. When she re-greased the probe and put it against my side, it was considerably colder than the first application. "You'd better stick that jelly back in the heater."

"Actually, most women say the same thing."

"Why is that? Not why do women say it, but is there some anatomical difference that causes the cold sensation on the left side?"

"We don't know for sure."

My analytical mind was whirring. "Could it be the gas?"

"Gas?"

"Yeah, the gas you found around my right side. Maybe the sound going through the gas creates heat."

"I don't know. I suppose it's possible."

"I guess farts collect on the right side, then. That would explain it."

"I'm sure I wouldn't know. Roll on your left side, please."

She took several more scanned images, then declared she was finished. As I sat up and wiped the goo from my abdomen and sides, I inquired, "Now that you've gotten about every angle of my innards scanned, will you create a 3-D composite for me? You know, kind of a hologram I can impress my friends with."

QUESTION OF THE DAY:

Can you cure kleptomania by taking a pill?

I don't want to sound like a philosophical moralistic nor a legalistic zero-tolerance advocate, yet I do wonder if thievery is ever excusable.

9

Brotherhood

Wow, today went by fast. My brother, Bob, is in town from Texas, so the three Kaiser boys spent the day together. Aside from the usual catching up, one significant dilemma was weighing heavily on Bob's mind. He needed closure on an issue… and possibly, absolution. His turmoil stemmed from a possible thievery of rhubarb.

When he first confessed this transgression, I wondered if there wasn't some Statute of Limitations on garden-plundering. His guilt feelings were from incidents occurring, or allegedly occurring, some 50 years ago. I'm not sure why Bob thought confession was necessary, but he needed to know whether Rick and I remembered jumping the fence to partake of the neighbor's rhubarb.

I was surprised that Rick didn't try to deny participation in such events on the grounds that Bob and I never took him anywhere. Yet, he did remember the rhubarb, but was sure there was no need for repentance, as the rhubarb was most certainly wild. Though it may indeed have grown outside the confines of our yard, Rick claimed its flavor was not typical of "garden rhubarb". He definitely remembered it had a wild taste. He confidently stated, "Surely, those plants could be considered as... well... sorta... growing free."

I disavowed any knowledge of, connection with, or responsibility for, anyone eating any rhubarb from the other side of any fence, though I did recall the fence and how easy it was to jump.

I also remembered Dad's compost barrel was positioned right next to the apple tree and just about the height of the fence. Hey, if we could jump off it, vaulting the fence wouldn't have violated Dad's prohibition of "climbing" the fence.

In addition to proposing *that* defense for Bob's coincident second offense, *I* categorically denied using the barrel to leap to the aforementioned rhubarb patch. In fact, I thought the rhubarb could be reached from our side of the fence, but both Rick and Bob insisted it could *not* be reached from our yard. Well, there you have it. I'm innocent. If I don't know where the subject plants were located, how could I possibly have been complicit in my brother's crime?

Bob wondered if we remembered Mom making a peace offering to the neighbors for the dubious acts of her sons. "Didn't she make an apple pie for them?" he asked. I guess he felt if she had, it would somehow vindicate him.

Nope, neither Rick nor I recalled any pies given to the neighbors in lieu of rhubarb. More evidence for Rick's and my innocence. If we didn't remember pies offered as restitution, we must be absolved of any culpability. Sorry Bob, you must bear your guilt alone. Shame on you.

But wait. Maybe you shouldn't feel guilty on this matter, Bob. This could be simply a matter of your subconscious mind trying to rationalize your present dislike for rhubarb pie. Maybe, fifty years ago, there was a mutual, neighborly exchange of apple pie for rhubarb. After all, if Mom had found out we'd taken rhubarb that didn't belong to us, it wouldn't have been pie in her grasp when she went to the neighbors. It would have been her son's ear, or ears, as the case may have been.

It's good that brothers can get together now and then to help each other through such distressing quandaries.

QUESTION OF THE DAY:

Can a fish live well in a live well?

It's not a live well, but we do want our fish to live well in our pond.

10

Winterizing

In the midst of one of our flower beds we have a pond. Kind of a decorative accent, not a big, natural, cattail-lined, lily-padded pond. Actually, it's more like a plastic puddle. It is large enough for a couple fish, though, and therein lies the challenge: how to keep them alive through the winter.

Natural ponds support fish through the winter, even though they freeze over. Not so with the plastic ponds. I've been advised to keep our pond from icing over, or the fish will suffocate.

So, I decided to keep the circulating pump running all winter. We route the pump discharge up through an antique hand-pump. With the first freeze, in early November, ice formed around the pond's periphery and in the shallow end, but the stream of water flowing out of the spout kept the center of the pond open. I was happy with the set-up.

Then the gale winds of November hit. Blustery gusts easily diverted the stream of the pump's discharge outside the pond.

In the summer, this is hardly a problem. High winds effectively water the surrounding flowers, and I just drag over the hose to replenish the pond to our desired depth. Not so in winter. November winds are far more frequent and significantly stronger than summer breezes. With plumbing to outside faucets shut off and no hose readily available, I was forced to haul pails of water from the basement source of un-softened water. The pond was losing 5 gallons a day. With that much water loss, I decided to cease the one-man bucket brigade and engineer a fix for the overspray at the pond.

Amid the organized rubble in my garage, I located a piece of coiled plastic. Remember those red plastic pseudo-toboggans that you had to unroll to ride down the hill? Well, I had one that would work perfectly to shield the stream of water from the spout to the pond.

It was easy to attach a wire to suspend the coiled plastic from the pump's snout. The ice-buildup from the splayed water had already formed a near-perfect support to maintain the necessary angle to keep the arched stream flowing freely within the two foot-diameter, pseudo pipe.

Unfortunately, November temperatures in Michigan do not stay below freezing. It wasn't long before a thaw melted the support and my shield swung straight down. That was not conducive to good water flow. A subsequent freeze solidified the water now splashing against the inside of my red cone. Once again the pond crusted over.

A hammer and ice pick opened everything back up, but I knew it was only a temporary remedy. To keep the red cone in place, I roughly framed it in with two-by-fours slung shore-to-shore across the pond. Voila! Back in business.

Oh, but when temperatures plummeted to sub zero, my meager pump's water pressure couldn't forestall frozen lines. A bigger pump was put into play. This time I did not route the submerged pump's discharge through tubing; its discharge erupted in the center of the pond.

Too much eruption. It created a virtual tsunami. The resultant waves were sufficient to again displace 5 gallons a day. Back to the garage for a new solution.

Ah-ha! I spotted a stack of plastic crates. Oh yeah! One of those plastic, milk crates would work to quell the tidal waves. I had crates of red, green and blue. I chose red, which sorta matched the rolled-up shield now firmly frozen to the two-by-fours as well as the iced-over pond at the far end.

I placed a chunk of wood on top of the crate to keep it slightly submerged and hovering over the gusher. The cross-hatched, lattice walls of the crate made a marvelous wave-deflector, plus, a fabulous foundation for some really awesome ice formations throughout the winter.

It is now Spring. The beautiful white snow-framing of the pond is gone. The ice sculptures melted. All that's left now are a few pieces of strewn lumber, a coiled-up red toboggan hanging from a rusty farm pump, and a grubby milk crate floating in the center of our pond. It looks more like a toxic-waste site than a decorative accent to our garden. Though the goldfish don't seem to mind the mess, it's time to get started with spring cleanup.

QUESTION OF THE DAY:

Why is it that night falls but it's the day that breaks?

The way it was back in the day compared to present day standards is as different as night and day, yet difficult to explain to the present generation. It's like explaining how swag has definitively changed from a form of drapery to the way your pants drape below the waist.

11

Back in the Day...

I'll just bet that you have received one of those nostalgic e-mails that remind you of how it was *back in the day*. Usually the point of those missives is that our lives back then were not only fabulously enjoyable, but somehow better for us. And before e-mail, parents often orated advice to their kids similarly... *when I was a boy, I walked to and from school... uphill both ways*. I know my dad intended such utterances to be a lesson for me.

Today, when Sue or I try to tell our grandkids what it was like *back in the day*, it usually ends up more laughable than a lesson. It's hard to keep a straight face while explaining the advantages we thought 8-track had over our teen norm of 45s to grandkids who have millions of, if not a gazillion, "records" on a pod that plays into a bud.

By the way, where'd the term "bud" come from? My guess is, whoever thought to call it a "bud" may have said something offensive after drinking a few too many "Buds" and was told to stick it in his ear.

Another 'in your ear' thing today is a 'blue tooth'. Aw, come on now… there's a marketing challenge. How do you put blue, tooth and ear in a catchy a slogan. Brings back my remembrance of "Nothing sucks like Electrolux".

Okay, so maybe half of you don't have a clue what an Electrolux is, or ever heard that advertising slogan. It was a vacuum cleaner which the slogan promoted as exceptionally powerful. In today's vernacular, a product which 'sucks' is not worth promoting. Coining a catchphrase for a 'A *blue tooth in your ear*' could be costly.

Let's face it… teeth and ears aren't even close together, and close together is precisely what I think Bluetooth technology enables. I'm not even sure that "close together" would work in marketing that product. It's a tough sell to encourage people to let a blue tooth anywhere near their ears. Pearly-white teeth, maybe, but blue teeth are not what I'd consider particularly romantic, and finding said nibblers near my ear would adversely stimulate me.

Yes, I know it's not sold from the pharmacy shelf with Cialis®. But thinking of being close together, teeth and ears did lead my mind astray.

Yes, I know that Bluetooth is a phone. Which brings up one last humorous comparison from back in my day to today's common place communications. When we tried to explain "party line" to our grand-kids, they could not relate.

Actually, neither can I. Considering that a bazillion conversations are floating through the air—not to mention aired publicly with cell phones, yet only a half-dozen went down the same party line long ago, it boggles my mind why "listening in" isn't more prevalent today than during the "party line" era.

But then, listening in isn't really hard to do with cell phones. Back in the day, girls would drag the phone, cord and all, into the bathroom for privacy. Today, I often overhear private conversations in the public bathroom stall next to me. A few times I've succumbed to the rebellious urge to enter into others' private, yet audibly public, conversations.

Such interruption was considered utterly rude on a party line. Now, with today's cellular Bluetooth technology, it's highly questionable as to which party can be called 'rude'.

QUESTION OF THE DAY:

If the #2 pencils are the most frequently used, why aren't they #1?

I love to shop. That's probably as 'un-macho' as asking directions, but I do that too. Actually, I am more of a buyer than a shopper. If I need a pencil, I go buy one, rather than walking through stores shopping for something to buy. I only shop to find the best deal for what I need. Sue on the other hand…

12

Pencil-Pusher

We often shop at SAM's Club. If you don't mind buying bigger quantities, there's usually quite a savings on some stuff. I got caught in the quantity syndrome the last time we went there to shop.

"Hey, Ed," Sue called, "Come over here." She wasn't at the jewelry counter, so I figured it was safe.

"We need pencils," She announced.

"Pencils? We need pencils?"

"Yes, and these 7-millimeter BicMatics are perfect."

"BicMatic?" My question was more of a stall than inquiring about the nature of the pencils. I was well aware that these were the lead pencil equivalent of a retractable ball point pen.

"Yes," she said as she handed me the package. "See, they've got the special grip."

"Special grip? Do you have a problem holding onto a pencil?"

"No. It's a comfort grip."

"Oh, gee… we certainly must pad our pinkies when we jot down the grocery list. Come on, let's go get the groceries."

"No. Wait, Ed. I've looked at Meijer's, and these mechanical pencils cost a lot more there."

"But there's 32 pencils in this package."

"I know, but we already have 7-millimeter leads at home. Remember we bought a million-pack a couple years ago."

"What happened to the pencils we bought that lead for?"

"I don't know." She shrugged off my bewildered question. "Look, there are at least 6 different colors in this value pack."

"There are thirty-two pencils in this value-pack. I worked 36 years at GM and never used up 32 pencils… refillable or not."

"But, Ed, they're only 8 dollars. That's only about a quarter a piece. We can't get them anywhere else that cheap."

I hate it when she's so fast with the math. It's intimidating. I saw the sign: $8.64.

My simplistic, non-calculating mind thought that was a bit much to fill our need for a pencil. When she so astutely pointed out we could get a pencil for a mere 27 cents, how could I refuse?

After tossing the value-pack in the shopping basket, I mused aloud; "I cannot imagine what happened to all of our pencils. We used to have them strewn everywhere around the house and a few in the car, too."

"I really don't know," came her nonchalant reply. "All I know is we're down to 6."

"DOWN TO SIX?!?!?" I retorted. "We're gonna buy 32 pencils and we've still got 6 at home?"

"But it seems like I can never find one when I need it."

I guess she won't have any trouble finding one now... and they were only a quarter apiece.

QUESTION OF THE DAY:

Do you think the medical profession should re-think their acronym for "Shortness of Breath"?

The medical profession provides me with many subjects for frivolous thinking. Advertising on TV is a wonderful source for provocative thought. I guess I shouldn't have been surprised that reading about my pills would be so entertaining. But then, I'm easily entertained.

13

Side Effects

The dictionary defines *Side Effect* as something which occurs in addition to an intended effect. The term is mostly applicable to medicines... which is exactly why it came to the forefront of my frivolous thoughts today.

In conjunction with a recent visit to my doctor, I decided to get a renewal on a prescription I had not needed for over a year. To get the right script, I retrieved the "Pharmacy Prescription Info Sheet". True to my nature, I perused the entire text of that document.

It's a med formulated to **"reduce itching, redness and swelling associated with many skin conditions"**. Perfect, that's the one I need. Further down the page it revealed possible side effects. **"When applied to the skin** (as if anyone would think to squeeze some on a toothbrush) **it may cause hives".**

Now, my *farm-acology* (not to be confused with a phonetically similar word) says the physiological interaction of hives and skin is itching. Hold on there, Bubba. I want the prescription 'cause my skin itches, not to *cause* it to itch.

Oh, but wait… just to clarify hives pharmacologically, it went on: **"may cause burning, itching and redness"**. No, I'm not making that up. The same cream that I wipe on a skin rash may cause a bigger rash… not to mention **"difficulty breathing, swelling of the mouth, face, lips or tongue"**.

Well, there you have it. No more itching on my arm, but my tongue swells up enough to choke me. They really didn't need to tell me to seek immediate medical attention if that occurred.

It seems that every medication now comes with disclaimers of detrimental side effects. I'm quite certain most of you have heard about the classic **"…lasting more than 4 hours…"** side effect. But, I think I'll not go there.

I'm not sure why side-effect disclaimers need to be the propriety of medications. Considering the recent barrage of political TV ads, I kept waiting for small print at the bottom to declare: **"May cause headache, nausea and vomiting"**, which, ironically, seems to be just about the most common side effect of prescription drugs.

Many meds warn: **"May cause drowsiness"**. I once got a script to help me overcome insomnia. It had the warning: **"Do not operate machinery or drive as it may cause drowsiness"**. Darn… you mean mowing the lawn is no longer an option when I can't sleep?

And why are all side effects negative? Just once I'd like to read a disclaimer that's favorable. Wouldn't it be great if Lopressor® reduced stomach acid build up in conjunction with its expressed purpose of reducing blood pressure? Oh, no, no, no… its side effects include both diarrhea AND constipation. That's kinda like a weather report of possible intermittent showers.

I take an anti-cholesterol pill every night. It would be nice if it had a positive side effect of drowsiness. Even better—the ultimate complementary side effect might be: **"Taking this medication may cause euphoria"**. Now there's a side effect I'd like to see on all my Prescription Info Sheets.

Oh, oh, but wait… Would the delightful side effect of euphoria become adverse if it lasts more than 4 hours?

QUESTION OF THE DAY:

Will listening for the bull keep you from getting hornswoggled?

Regardless of what you think hornswoggled is, it seems rather easy to discover the bull in most government issued notices. This is especially evident when explaining the rationale for laws, regulations and ordinances.

14

Wetlands Ordinance

I am not a lawyer, nor do I have much success interpreting legalese. I suppose that I am not particularly unusual in that regard. When government entities are required to advise their constituents of the effects of a legal action, they might be expected to write those explanations in terms the general public has a chance of comprehending. I recently received one such letter, but, it caused me more confusion than comprehension.

I received a "**NOTICE OF ADOPTION—WETLAND PROTECTION ORDINANCE**" from my township office. Paragraph one was a cinch to interpret. Hey, even a dummy could understand that "**...the ordinance provides for the protection of wetlands**" means the WETLAND PROTECTION ORDINANCE is exactly as its name suggests.

That's good to know, as sometimes the governmental masterminds hide all manner of foolishness under innocent-sounding names. Also in the first paragraph was the definitive clarification that "**this** [Wetlands

Protection] **Ordinance applies to wetlands**". Well, hellooo, that was categorically a no-brainer paragraph.

Even paragraph two, with the inclusion of a legalistic delineation; **"Part [this] of Act [that], provision [something-or-other] in 1994"**, was not so complex to forestall my understanding. And I was stride-for-stride with them when the letter mentioned they were required to advise me that my property **"may be designated as a wetland"**.

In paragraph three, I was even able to clear the first hurdle of discernment of convoluted text. Just because my property may not be **"...designated wetland... on the inventory map"**, I cannot just jump to the conclusion that I'm exempt from the ordinance's regulating power because **"...the inventory map does not necessarily include all of the wetlands"**. It was tricky with all the commas and prepositions, but I managed to sort out the import of paragraph three. No *absolute* is discernible from the map alone.

Then I started to stumble. Not only is there no absolute, the letter went on to admit the map isn't **"legally enforceable"**. Why go to the trouble to tell me about a map that may misidentify my sandy hilltop property as wetlands, or negligently overlook the swamp a half-mile away, if said map cannot be enforced?

I won't bother to quote the entire letter, but it went on to explain that the map might have designated some property as wetlands that are not definitively a bog, marsh, or even moist, spongy soil. But I really got tripped up by what seemed to be an admission that they just might have missed putting a swamp or two on the map.

Additionally, such an omission should not be confused with whether the land is actually considered **wetlands**. Furthermore, it seems that all of the **wetlands,** within the township, may not be subject to the ordinance.

I feel like somebody took the balloon out of my carotid artery. Why did they bother to tell me that I *may or may not* have wetlands on my property that *may or may not* be on a map that *may or may not be accurate?* Certainly I should not make presumptions from it, because the map doesn't mean squat to the ordinance. [*Note:* "Squat", per se, did not appear anywhere in the letter yet the idea seemed abundant throughout.]

Ahhhh, but guess what? I can inspect this worthless map during regular business hours. Although visiting the township office **during regular business hours** effectively precludes me from secretly erasing my pond from the map, what difference would it make if I could sneak in after-hours? Regardless of my pond (actually only a vision at present) being on the map or not… whether my property is actually wet or even **"contiguous"** to something wet (hmmm, I wonder how many miles wide *contiguous* is)… no matter if my land has a low spot which spans a half-acre or not, this Wetland Protection Ordinance might still affect me.

Okay, who thinks I should call the township office for clarification of this matter?

QUESTION OF THE DAY:

Supposedly, diamonds are a girl's best friend... why does a man have to settle for a dog?

This question has troubled me for a long time. And it's not because I have any aversion to dogs. Why can't a man's best friend be a car, or his tools, or at least a Captain America Decoder Ring. Dog should be reclassified as a kid's best friend. I've enjoyed all the dogs I have had, but sometimes... not as a best friend.

15

Fermentation

I've heard that the human aging process is like that of producing fine wine. Of course, the thought is most often expressed from a positive perspective. I've found it equally applicable at most every stage; from grapes on the vine to enchanting extract, especially in the context of memory.

This fermentation of memory is often evident when I share a story with Sue. If the saga is from the distant past, the wine is savory. However, if I'm trying to recall something I heard on the radio yesterday, it's more like souring grape juice than a sparkling libation.

The other day, I found the wine analogy to have another ironic association. Perusing a news release uncorked a somewhat fermented memory from many years ago. The ironic recall was stimulated by the news report on a dog's discovery of an object on the beach with a repulsive aroma. Wiggles, our dog of the 80s, had not only discovered such an object, but wallowed in it.

At home, if Wiggles realized we were watching him, he 'knew' his boundaries and rarely violated them. No need for a leash for his potty break so long as we were in his sight. While camping, however, he recognized no boundary, so a leash was imperative. On one particular outing, each of us thought Wiggles was leashed to the camper, excitedly prancing around our feet as we finished packing up to head home.

As I recall, we didn't realize he had left the campsite until his return was pungently announced. Possibly he had gone to the beach to defecate. The stench deeply embedded in his fur suggested he had either forgotten to take toilet paper with him, or he had deeply investigated some other form of "waste".

So, you ask, how does this historic tale relate to the news release? The news article was about a dog discovering excrement on a beach… specifically whale vomit. Initially that dog's discovery was as repulsive to the owner as the evidence of Wiggles' discovery was to us. However, there are three significant differences between his story and mine.

First, the man's dog found a dried mass. Wiggles' find was in much earlier stages of decomposition.

Which leads to the second difference: the man went back to retrieve the dried mass while I was tempted to leave both Wiggles and his discovery right then and there.

Now, however, I'm wondering if I might have been richer—in both cents and scents—if I had followed Wiggles back to the source. It seems that whale vomit is worth about fifty grand a pound. Perfume manufacturers utilize it to prolong the bouquet of their product. Go figure.

But alas, we had camped at an inland lake. No whales. Not to mention that we had absolutely no desire to prolong Wiggles' *bouquet*. With Joy… not particularly mine nor Wiggles' but that which comes in a bottle, I emulsified the pollutants in his fur and *fresh-scented* the mutt. Like fine wine, my memory of Wiggles' encounter with something sourly fermented has sweetened over time.

QUESTION OF THE DAY:

Can you actually draw a blank?

Even though my Question of the Day is typically rhetorical, a question from Sue frequently inspires a very blank look on my face. This occurs most often when her question is answerable, yet I should refrain from doing so.

16

What's This?

"Hey, Ed, what's this?"

That would be Sue calling to me from the kitchen.

Now, I immediately realize this question is not posed because of her lack of knowledge. If she didn't know the answer, her question would be prefaced with, "That's strange." *"What's this?"* for Sue is like an only child's mother asking *"Who did this?"* She knows; she's just baiting a trap.

So I don't step blindly into the trap; I cautiously follow up with "What's *what?*"

On the surface, it's a really dumb response, but it should suffice as a stall—an essential one as my mind retraces my last activity in the kitchen. What did I leave open? I'm always harassing Sue about leaving open cupboard doors and drawers, or stove burners on. That can't be it. This morning my only forage into the kitchen was to get an orange from the fridge. That door closes by itself. I eagerly await her next clue.

"This, that I found in the microwave."

Scrrreeeech... that would be the sound of stressing steel in the trap. Kind of a metallic excitement of the spring about to uncoil and cold-cock an unsuspecting victim. Though hardly unsuspecting at this point, the victim's identity is painfully obvious. Me.

You see, there are no grandkids present, so I have no scapegoat. Even *my* feeble logic readily concludes: if *she* had left it in the microwave, *she* wouldn't be asking the question.

However, I'm still a bit puzzled. Regardless of my often ineffectual logic, my memory of this morning is very clear. Pills, and one orange from the fridge. Even Goofy Ed doesn't nuke pills or oranges... nor did I use the microwave for any other purpose this morning. I'm baffled as to what she's found.

As I round the corner into the kitchen... SNAP! The trap is sprung. "Do you think this has steeped long enough?" Sue asks with a noticeably accusatory inflection while holding a not-so-steamy cup of tea. "Ed, if you want cold tea, why put it in the microwave in the first place?"

The worst? This was not an event of *this* morning that escaped my recollection.

Yesterday I put that tea in to heat. Would you believe, I'm quite fond of ambient, strong tea? Honest... the scum doesn't bother me a bit.

I didn't think you'd believe it.

Well then, how 'bout—I leave it to steep overnight to ensure getting every bit of flavor from each tea bag?

Nah, probably not that either. Okay... so I flat-out forgot. I know you'd believe that.

I honestly don't understand why this happens so frequently. I'm not ADD and I'm not easily distracted. Moreover, I'm a creature of habit. I take pills every morning from a dozen different bottles—often with my eyes closed—without missing a dose. I'm generally very systematic and purposeful. Nevertheless, it's even odds I will fail to retrieve my tea within the hour.

However, the *hour* in which I typically retrieve it seems to be coincident with the next use of the microwave.

QUESTION OF THE DAY:

If it's illegal to even stop, why does the sign also include 'no standing or parking'?

I can recall seeing this questionable sign when I was a very small boy. My dad & I were waiting for mom to 'run into the store for a minute'. As my father crept the old Dodge along the street, I asked why he was travelling so slowly. He pointed to the sign; "I can't stop or park here and standing means not moving, so I must idle along to avoid a ticket." Even my adolescent mind knew enough not to ask if mom was going to have to jump into the moving car. Even to this day, the sign baffles me.

17

Roadside Signs

It's quite amazing what captivates my mind when traveling. Aside from my astonishment at natural formations and historical sites, man-made things also fascinate me. Sometimes, even a simple thing like a sign jerks at my mind like a dog yanking on an old sock.

Though there are often thought-provoking commercial signs, the ones that often truly astound me are the Highway Department and municipal signs. I could not help but wonder who thought it was necessary to stab a "DO NOT MOW" sign into the sheer, solid rock cliff jutting up abruptly a mere foot from the shoulder of the road. My weed-eater would starve looking for grass there.

Okay, so it's possible someone placed that sign there as a practical joke. It worked. Sue and I both got a chuckle out of it. However, some signs exist which are not intended as jokes, yet amuse me. Amuse, that is, in a burlesque sort of way.

"FALLING ROCKS". What sense is that? In the present tense, its credibility wanes with my experience. And even if one of those strategically-placed warnings did prove to be prophetic, what options do I have at 70 miles an hour? Especially considering the sign is plural.

So, you say, my best option is to slow down and be especially observant of the rocky slope? If all vehicles did likewise, we'd have gridlock on the mountainside. Even a single stone dislodged from the precipice would have overwhelming odds of hitting someone's car in the bumper-to-bumper parade.

Ah, but some states have opted to word the sign "FALLEN ROCKS". I am eternally grateful for this grammatical correction. Most certainly I could have driven for many miles wondering just what that debris was off to the right. Without such edifying signage I might have mistaken the rocks for a herd of turtles, petrified by their fear of being run over.

One last sign's importance I wonder about. I've now visited a half-dozen states which have enacted laws mandating vehicles "STOP for PEDESTRIANS in CROSSWALK". And they've got a million signs to prove it. The sensibility of this message escapes me. If there's no sign, go ahead and run 'em down?

I'll admit, I've been tempted to apply vehicular natural selection to teens who defiantly amble down the middle of the street, but shall I hit one just because there isn't a sign to protect them? Give me a break. I may be goofy, but I'm not stupid.

As for the feasibility of protecting cross-walkers, of what significance are the signs from the pedestrian point of view? I gotta tell ya, my pedestrian point of view would be stationary, on the curb—sign or no sign—until I found a substantial gap in traffic. A car at dead stop would work also. My jaywalking ability is inversely proportion to my age. At my age, my agility is comparable to a duck on ice.

My caution as a pedestrian, even in the states with signs proclaiming the law, comes from my driving experience. Much like the "FALLING ROCKS" sign, nobody really drives any differently with or without these state law reminders. If pedestrians are not obviously crossing, I maintain whatever speed is allowed. Conversely, if I see pedestrians leaning into the roadway—or rocks falling—I don't need the signs to tell me what to do.

Save money. Stop making these signs. Nobody changes the way they drive because of them.

On second thought, keep making the signs. I appreciate the entertainment.

QUESTION OF THE DAY:

Does anyone know what it's like to be in whack?

I have no idea where whack is… nor have I been in cognito either. However, it has been rumored that I've been in cahoots more than once. In the matter of being in or out of whack, I do not understand how being out of whack was derived from getting hit. I suppose, if out of whack is indicative of being disabled, then my mind has long since left that location.

18

Muscle Strain

I injured my leg this week. Softball. Church league softball. You'd think with all the praying before the game, there'd be a lot fewer injuries in a Church league.

Hmmm, you don't suppose that my sore calf is God's answer to the pre-game prayer; "…and Lord, keep us mindful of why we're here." (or shouldn't be, as the case may be for me?)

Anyway, during the game this week, something popped in my calf when I lurched for a grounder. Did I think of the physical reality that old muscles do not take kindly to sudden hyper-extensions? NOT.

It was not immediately debilitating, though. I didn't fall on my face, like in last week's game, when my hamstring harshly objected to chasing a ground ball. It was the next morning that my aching calf muscle objected to anything more strenuous than crawling.

So, I decided maybe an ice pack would sooth the ache. Have you ever put an ice pack on your calf? Sitting on the couch, my resources for holding the ice pack in place were considerably limited. The towel I'd chosen was too short to tie a knot, but maybe my belt would suffice. I removed it from my shorts, wrapped the freezer-pack in the towel, and strapped it to my lower leg.

Not bad! The coolness was already starting to soothe the ache. The coolness abruptly dissipated when I stood up. Both my shorts and the ice pack slipped well below a functional level.

Did I mention that it was my calf muscle; did I think of the physical reality that, as I bent forward to strap on the ice pack, my calf muscle was tensed and therefore enlarged? NOT.

I sat back down, put my leg up on the couch to relieve all muscle tension in the calf, and wound the belt tighter. Reaching to my calf with my leg straight stretched the hamstring. Ouch! That brought a quick reminder of where the ice pack had been after last week's game.

So, now I've got the ice pack in place, belted tightly to my lower leg. I got up to go answer some e-mail. First step... thump. Down goes the ice pack again. I quickly grabbed my shorts in one hand and bent my knees to grab the ice pack as it slithered toward my ankle.

Did I mention the injury was in my calf? Did I think of the physical reality that my calf muscle stretches to painful limits when squatting to pick up fallen ice packs? NOT.

So I gave up on belting the ice pack in place; I just let it drag until I got to the computer. Then I pulled up a chair next to me at the computer, placed the toweled ice pack on it and hoisted my leg up onto the chair. Ahhh, that felt good. Success. Though it was a bit awkward to have my left leg at 45 degrees to the side, I was able to read the e-mail and type responses.

Did I mention that the chair I chose to prop my leg on was somewhat higher in elevation than the one I was sitting on? Did I think of the physical reality that blood does not circulate well through 45-degree hip bends and uphill? NOT.

It wasn't long before my toes were colder than the ice pack, not to mention that the splits and elevation had put my butt to sleep.

Of course, we all know the physical reality of what causes our limbs to "fall asleep": It's pinched nerves. Not only was my fanny numb, the nerves to my calf were also deadened. Relief!

Why had I bothered with the ice pack? I should have just used my belt as a tourniquet on the sciatic nerve.

QUESTION OF THE DAY:

What happens if you get scared half to death twice?

There are many commonly used phrases which have commonly understood implications. The problem is that my mind uncommonly twists the interpretation of what people say. It's not so much a problem for me, as for them. Their extemporaneous phrasing typically generates twisted responses from me.

19

Prompted by Poor Phrasing

Yesterday, Sue was scheduled for her third lithotripsy in 6 months. (Lithotripsy is a procedure to blast kidney stones with sound waves.)

In preparation for that procedure, Sue took a wheelchair ride down to X-ray while I waited in her pre-op cubicle. A few moments later, a nurse passed by the cubicle, glanced at the empty bed, then at me. "Oh, are you with someone?"

I kindly responded, "Nah, it's cold outside, and I thought I'd just sip this coffee and watch the morning news."

She chuckled, and continued; "The curtain was open, and we usually keep it closed when the room is occupied."

"Aw, don't worry about me. I don't need the privacy."

"I meant, when the room is occupied by a patient."

I started to point out that the patient was not currently occupying the room, but the nurse had already closed the curtain on our dialogue.

She left shaking her head, no doubt wondering about my sanity. Maybe she should have wondered about the sensibility of her questions— and follow-up explanations—rather than my demented responses which she evoked from my deranged mind. What seemed logical to her, I found semantically irrational. Or at least, poorly-phrased.

Yeah, I know… picky! picky! But that's who I am. Such phraseology often puts my demented mind in a frenzy.

When the x-ray, and subsequent ultra-sound, could not find any stone to fire a laser at, the doctor sent Sue home.

She was hungry, so we stopped at BurgerWhop for her favorite chicken sandwich. When I drove up to the order station, a voice greeted me, "Can I take your order?"

BZZZPT! That's the sound of my brain short-circuiting. Often I respond to this grammatical miscue with a snappy remark about not being qualified to judge the voice's physical capabilities. Often, that is, in social settings where I know the person who used "can" instead of "may". However, I didn't know the person taking my order, so I resisted that temptation.

Instead I simply ordered one Original Chicken Sandwich, though I wondered what could be so *original* about a chicken sandwich. The voice responded in an uncharacteristic, rather casual tone, "Well… let's see… okay… How about… four ninety-six."

I could not help myself. "Is that negotiable?"

The voice was baffled by my rejoinder. As he searched for words, I told him never mind, and drove up to the pick-up window. When I got there, he was smiling. "It took me a minute, but now I know what you meant."

Some of them never catch on, though. Sometimes when the voice at the order station directs: "That will be eight ninety-eight at the first window," I respond with, "Will I get a better price at the second window?"

It's not just voices at remote-order stations that are baffled by my comebacks. The other day, a department store check-out girl asked: "May I have your phone number?"

"Shhh, my wife's standing right here. I'll call *you*."

The cashier's puzzled expression clearly indicated she did not comprehend my inference.

Even Sue gets caught up in asking poorly-phrased questions. Once, she noticed me on a ladder, cleaning the downspout in the middle of a heavy rain. "What are you doing now?" she shouted. Considering the overflow from the eaves was filling my pants, I wanted to answer, "Taking a shower!"

But, I suppose Sue's familiar with my abnormal norms, so questions like "What are you doing?" do not necessarily reflect her lack of observation. Rather, they question my lack of rational thinking.

QUESTION OF THE DAY:

How do you decide whether to give up, or give in?

The answer to this question is not only hypothetical, it is also moot... as in little or no practical value, when applied to a project which Sue proposes.

20

Teeny-Tiny Job

Sue's latest little project is making Barbie Doll furniture out of yarn. Lately she has been working in the bathroom. No, not our bathroom… though it does need some work. What I meant was, she's been working in the Barbie Bathroom.

Now, you'd think that I'd be exempt from this little project. Yarn and Barbie are not exactly my bailiwick. At least I *thought* I'd be exempt.

The other day Sue came seeking my assistance in cutting plastic. I figured cutting was in line with my skill level, so I agreed. Then she handed me a tiny, quarter-inch plastic, berry-bead ball; "See this ring?"— indicating a circle of five infinitesimal orbs encircling one end of the tiny ball. "I need it."

"You're kidding, right? Those beads aren't even a millimeter in diameter."

"Maybe you can wedge an X-acto blade between the rings and pry them apart. I think the glue is pretty weak."

"I think your glue's gettin' a bit weak, too. What do you need these itty bitty rings of beads for?"

"Don't you think they'll look like old-fashioned glass knobs for the shower?"

"Are you serious? I can only imagine what I'll be cutting out for the faucet."

"Never mind that right now. Just try to get these balls apart for me. You see, there's a plastic shaft right down the middle of the ball. All you have to do is loosen the glue, and I think the ends will pop right off."

Oh, yeah… I could see the shaft, all right… but off I went to my sanctuary of self-sacrifice. My workshop is often where I can go for some solitude. It is also where I often inflict wounds which bleed on the workbench altar.

Trying to wedge an X-acto blade between objects barely visible to the naked eye seems like a sure bet for a little blood-letting. Barbie stuff is pink, though, not mottled red. So it's indeed fortunate that the blood didn't stain the plastic. Incredibly, by the time I'd extricated the required eight beaded rings, I had only wounded two fingers.

I proudly marched upstairs with my completed task.

Sue thanked me and showed me the toilet she was now weaving together. "Have you got a heavy bolt about 2 inches long?"

"Geez, please don't tell me you're gonna bolt the toilet to the floor."

"Well... sort of. The back of the toilet is too heavy for the stool. It keeps tipping over backwards."

"Yeah, and I imagine it will be even worse when it's full of water."

"Don't be silly. You don't put water in this toilet."

"Whew, for a minute there I thought you'd be soon asking for 1-millimeter chrome tubing."

"Ed, just tell me if you've got the bolt or not. I need it to counterbalance the toilet."

So I got her the bolt.

"Great," she said. "Now all I need to do is wrap it."

"Wrap it!?! Why in the world do you need to wrap the bolt?"

"So the kids don't... you know..."

"Oh, suuuure... I understand. You surely wouldn't want them to take it out of the toilet bowl and put it in their mouths."

QUESTION OF THE DAY:

While you're driving and it rains for only a short time, is it a scattered or intermittent shower?

Traveling is one of the great joys of retirement. We enjoy visits to historical sites as well as stops to observe the wonderful scenery America has to offer. Whether visiting scenic grandeur or famed places, my wonderment often takes a side trip.

21

Pioneering

As Sue and I travel, we explore our country's rich heritage and magnificent natural geological formations. In our recent visits to sites in the southwest, we often questioned the mentality of Pioneers.

For example, imagine a pioneer father approaching his son, who's playing at the pond with a roughly-carved piece of wood—to him, a boat. "Come on, son, let's go. We're all packed and ready to head west."

"Can I take my boat, Dad?"

"No, son, there's aren't any ponds where we're going."

"No ponds? How 'bout a river?"

"Nope. Just washes."

"Well, if I can wash in it, I can float my boat."

"These 'washes' don't have water in them. It's a name for an area where water might collect if it rains."

"If it don't rain, how do trees grow?"

"No trees. Just wide, open spaces. Hundreds and hundreds… and hunnnnndreds of miles of dry, windswept space."

"If it's so dry, how we gonna grow crops, Dad?"

"We're not, son. We're just going to keep going until we find painted deserts, petrified trees, majestic rock formations, or magnificent canyons. When we find one of those, that's where we'll settle. We'll establish a park, set up some souvenir stands and make a fortune."

Okay, so maybe there weren't many pioneer dads that actually thought people would come by the millions to see rocks. However, you still have to wonder about the sanity of people who ventured away from the fertile East, especially if their routes went through north Texas, New Mexico and Arizona. About a week or two wandering in those states probably had the kids questioning when they would get to "the better life".

Oh, but when they came up on places like the Painted Desert, Grand Canyon, Arches, Bryce, and Zion (just to name a few places we visited) they certainly must have been in awe. SPECTACULAR is an understatement.

And *if* a pioneer dad *had* envisioned selling petrified trees, his descendents have sold me about 40 pounds. It was cheaper to buy the petrified wood outside the National Park than to "collect" such beautiful stones inside the park and face a stiff fine. In our rock garden, they'll be splendid reminders of the extraordinary magnificence of the Southwest.

QUESTION OF THE DAY:

Have you ever had an idea double cross your mind?

It is rather common for someone to say; "That did cross my mind". I cannot begin to tell you how many times I wished that would have happened for me. All too often my thought processes double cross me.

22

Chainsaw Massacre

My chainsaw stopped as I was cutting down the lilac in our yard. The saw is electric, so I checked the plug at the back—connected.

[*Note to a grandchild who demonstrates DIY characteristics similar to what mine were at his age, but does not yet fully understand electricity:* I use the term "plug" generically for either end of the electrical extension cord. There are colloquial terms which differentiate those connecting devices, but we will discuss those differences when you are older.]

I checked the plug at the house outlet—connected. I checked the "brake" on the saw—not engaged. I disconnected the electricity at the back of the saw and tried to move the chain using a stick.

[*Note to grandchild:* Regardless of apparent lack of electricity to the saw, always disconnect the power source.]

The chain wouldn't budge. So, I figured a branch had become wedged in the chain blades. Sometimes the green suckers of the lilac rip off rather than saw off cleanly. I thought maybe one of the suckers could have wedged where the chain entered the saw's housing.

Low and behold *something* was wedged there, but it was orange, not green... and not only was it wedged, it was half-severed... thus the loss of power.

Now I was quite upset. I had purposely looped the orange power cord over a branch above my head to preclude that from happening. No, I'm not so foolish to have cut that particular branch off yet. Apparently though, as I pulled a different severed "limb" from the bush, the cord had pulled loose from its safety perch.

So, now I must fix the cord. Fortunately the split was only a foot or so from the end of the 50-foot cord. Definitely worth salvaging. Such a repair job is a simple task.

[*Note:* Simple because the wires are different colors and attached with screws. Simply reattach color for color.]

I dragged the partially-severed end to my workbench in the garage and inserted my wire cutters into the damaged area. I squeezed the jaws of the cutters to cut the black wire at the same spot the saw had cut the white wire. As soon as the jaws cut through the insulation of the black wire, sparks flew.

[*Note:* Sparks are not a good thing when working with electricity. They indicate that electricity is objecting to whatever connection you have inadvertently made.]

Just because the saw wouldn't work with the white lead severed, that is not conclusive evidence that the lead is not *hot*—as in carrying current just waiting for the circuit to be connected. The metal jaws of the wire cutters effectively connected the white and black wires.

[*Note:* There's a purpose for wires to be different colors and it's not for artistic or aesthetic reasons. They are not intended to be connected to each other.]

Before continuing with repair of the extension cord, I disconnected the plug at the house outlet.

[*Note:* Regardless of apparent lack of electricity to the saw, always disconnect the power source. Hmmm, seems that I stated that earlier, yet failed to heed my own advice.]

I went to where the extension cord was plugged into the outlet at the back of the house and belatedly pulled the plug.

Back at my workbench, I finished severing the cord, disassembled the outlet and removed the white, black and ground wires of the now dysfunctional stub of the extension cord. I stripped the insulation from wires on the good end of the power cord.

Then Sue came into the garage to see what I was doing. After hearing my humbling admission to accidently cutting the cord instead of branches, she could hardly wait to go back into the house to proclaim my fallibility to the grandkids while I returned to my work on the bench.

It's a rather simple task to thread the orange cord into the disassembled outlet socket and tighten down the individual strands of wire, being careful to attach white to bright, black to brass and ground to green.

[*Note:* This is a standard saying of electricians—white wire to the bright colored screw-post, black wire to the brass screw and the ground wire (usually with no colored insulation) to the green screw.]

With all the wires appropriately attached, I reassembled the outlet. Job done.

Not.

Somehow, while I talked with Sue, the good end of the power cord had slithered off my bench and on to the floor. I had reconnected the stub end to the outlet.

So, now I must repair my repair—a rather common occurrence for me.

Repair of a repair is also a rather simple task—disassemble the outlet fixture, remove the wires of the stub end, and throw the stub end in the trash (which I obviously should have done much earlier in the repair process.)

Eventually I finished the rather simple task a second time and dragged the cord back to the lilac bush. After plugging the repaired end of the cord into the chain saw, I pulled the trigger to test the effectiveness of my repair.

Except for a blue jay laughing, there was silence. No whir of the motor to confirm a successful repair.

Did I mention that I had disconnected the cord at the house outlet? Ah, yes. Gotta plug that back in. With that accomplished, I went back to the saw and pulled the trigger… Nothing.

Did I mention the sparks that flew when I first began the repair process? Ah, yes. Gotta reset the circuit breaker. Honestly, I think a circuit was broken in my brain that afternoon as well.

QUESTION OF THE DAY:

Why is a wise guy so different than a wise man?

Some people seem to be blessed with wisdom. The extent of my wisdom is essentially limited to simplistic realities like; When you're upset, don't try to slam a revolving door. I will say that 70 years of experience is improving my good judgment—and a lotta that improvement came from bad judgment. Nevertheless, habit trumps judgment as this story clearly points out.

Powerless to Faux Pas

Winter... a beautiful season. Also a power-outage season. Ice storms, nor'easters, and heavy, wet snows frequently cause sapless brittle limbs to snap. Often I wonder if the power lines create a negative force-field which broken limbs cannot resist. Intermingling of wood and wire often causes the lights to go out.

We lost electrical power at least a dozen times this year. For one stretch of four weeks this past summer, we lost power every Thursday. After two outages in a row, Sue and I left town on the following Wednesday. By the time we returned on Saturday, ten days later, the power had gone off twice more... on Thursdays, and had just been restored. Now I'd call that a phenomenon.

Another phenomenon frequently occurs when the lights go out. We turn them on, anyway. Hey, it's dark. When I go into a room in the dark, I flip on the switch. Unfortunately, the light does not go on in the room nor my brain. Usually I leave the switch on.

This deficiency is compounded in our basement. We have 3-way switches there. Heading downstairs to get candles, I turn the switch on... which predictably fails to illuminate the basement. With my brain also in a black-out, I get to the bottom of the steps and flip *that* switch too. Ah-hah, you say. What's the problem? I have just turned off the circuit. All should be well.

Well? No.

You see (figuratively of course, as it's still very dark), I have the distinct habit of flipping the switch at the top of the stairs each time I ascend from the basement, also a habit which runs roughshod over the logic of why I'm carrying a lit candle.

Invariably, when power is restored, more lights are on in the house than off.

Another rather strange occurrence during black-outs involves water. My brain waves don't even ripple the pond. I know that our water is supplied by an electrical pump. That's the primary reason why one of my first vocalized cautions is regarding the water in the toilet.

No! I am not particularly worried about flushing, per se. At least the first flush would evacuate the waste, but there might not be sufficient re-supply water to fill the trap. Nor would there be electricity to energize the exhaust fan, and thus, no effective means to evacuate the aroma wafting up from the now open line to the septic tank. Not to mention the "Plug In" fragrance isn't currently empowered.

Trust me, no aerosol outlasts a power outage. Don't flush! There is no water.

But, if I knew that water wasn't available, why did I lather up my face when we decided to go out for dinner? I had realized the futility (if not pain), of trying to rip out whiskers with the stationery blades my non-electrified razor. Regrettably, my logic failed to equate "no water for the toilet" with "no water to rinse the Trac II® razor" after I had taken the first swipe.

I grabbed a towel and wiped my face clean, contemplating going out with a 5-o'clock-shadow. I don't know why I was squinting at the mirror, I didn't need to *see* the *shadowless* path in my whiskers, I could *feel* it. I lathered again and completed the process without the benefit of rinse. I can only hope Sue understands the little black flecks on the towel after the shaving cream evaporates.

After all, I understand her slip-up when we discussed dinner. She audibly pondered a simple meal, "I know we don't have water, so I can't make soup & sandwiches. But we do have some leftovers in the fridge. How about I warm them up in the micro... ahhhh, I mean... why don't we go out to eat?"

Isn't it phenomenal how the norms of life resist alteration by reality?

QUESTION OF THE DAY:

Would a crazy person take a psycho path for a walk?

Often our vacation itinerary includes a stop at a waterfall or two. Though some are adjacent to parking lots, many are only accessed by taking a path to the base of the falls. Usually, as we descend down the path, our excitement ascends as the cascading water becomes louder. Usually, but not always.

24

Waterfalls

Fall travel certainly has its advantages. Fewer vacationers on the road mean fewer sightseers to jostle with at scenic locations. And that scenery is generally more colorful than other times of the year, especially waterfalls. The splendor of fall colors framing crystalline-white water cascading over a rocky cliff is magnificent.

We had mapped out several such falls on our way to Atlanta, the first being Indian Falls. Sue had gotten directions from a couple of sites on the Internet. Both sites described Indian Falls as being in Alabama's DeSoto State Park. Unfortunately, they did not exactly agree on *where* within the park the falls were located. So, despite following the textual directions of both web pages, we couldn't find the falls. Our usually reliable GPS had no idea where Indian Falls was, either.

Did I mention that autumn is noticeably lacking in tourism? That equates to a lack of open tourist traps, as well as early closing of State Park information booths. No locals to ask how to get to the falls… more frustration. Ah, but we were able to secure a fairly detailed map from the porch of the abandoned park office. Considering the maps were stacked on a table beneath a rock, I assumed they were left for off-season park visitors by the gone-for-the-winter Park Rangers.

The maps were detailed, but hand-drawn, and not to scale, and north was not up—and where's my magnifying glass when I need it? All of which seemed to belie my assumption that the maps were left by rangers. More likely, they were created by winter maintenance workers who tired of giving directions to off-season visitors.

Regardless of who created the maps or why, once we became oriented, the map led us to the parking area for Azalea Cascades, directly across the street from a trail to Indian Falls.

I should have gotten the hint that this wouldn't be a particularly enjoyable excursion when we had to go around a waste treatment plant to get to the falls. We sensed a second hint of pending disappointment when the bridge near the falls was essentially spanning leaves—very colorful leaves, but precious little water.

The sign identifying the waterfall was large enough to obscure our view of the trickle of water. Drool would have more substance than this waterfall. Oh, the web site description was accurate: Indian Falls was a picturesque, twenty-foot drop amidst mountain laurel. Unfortunately the 20 feet was nearly sufficient to evaporate all the water before it hit bottom. We debated waiting for the sewage plant to cycle. Maybe that would produce enough effluent to make Indian Falls worth seeing.

But darkness was fast approaching, and we had Azalea Cascades yet to see. That trail led us upstream. Now, just why I thought that sites upstream from a nearly non-existent waterfall would be better escapes me. Maybe it was the boardwalk rather than a rocky path around a waste treatment plant. I had an image of the boardwalk leading to a different river, stream, creek, spring-fed brook… anything bigger than a leaky faucet. Alas, after walking a hundred feet up the boardwalk, my imaginings dried up, too. We saw nothing but Azalea leaves cascading.

Actually, even dried-up cascades and drizzling waterfalls have endearing qualities to us. We will definitely remember this adventure.

QUESTION OF THE DAY:

Why do we have a general in charge of the Post Office and a secretary in charge of Defense?

Regardless of the rank or empowerment of individual representatives of such agencies as the Postal Service, I delight in confronting such authority with simplistic logic.

25

An Encounter with USPS

It might be very good cookware, but T-fal cannot free-fall from the hands of a 6'4" klutz and survive unscathed. I checked the web for info on how to get a new handle. Believe it or not, there were no T-fal sites that would sell me a handle. My only option was to send it to their Customer Service Center. I packed it up and headed for the Post Office.

As I set the package on the counter, I inquired, "How much to ship this?"

"What is it?" the clerk asked pleasantly.

I explained, "It's a broken cooking pot that I need to send in for repair."

"Do you want to insure it?"

"Not hardly. It's broken. Can't use it like it is, so why insure it?"

"Because, if it gets lost, you can collect the money to replace it."

"Okay, how much to insure it?"

"How much is it worth?"

"Nothing. It's broken."

"Then that will be $1.35 minimum charge."

"You want me to pay a buck thirty-five to insure something that's worthless to me in its present state?"

"Well, Ed," (She knew me… I've been there before), "it's just an option I needed to suggest. How about putting a trace on the package?"

"A trace? It's right there. It has zero value. What's to trace?"

"If you don't purchase a trace on it, the company could claim they never got it."

"So? It's no good to me like it is. It's just like with the insurance. If they don't get it, or if they claim they don't get it, it's no different than if they won't fix it."

"Well, Ed, the Postal Service recommends traces for packages in situations like this."

"How much for a trace?"

"Fifty cents."

"Okay. I'll take the trace."

"Let's see… First Class, with Trace, that will be $7.95."

"I don't need First Class. Isn't there a cheaper way to send it?"

"If you don't send it First Class, instead of 2-day delivery, it might not get there for a week."

"What do I care? It's not like we need this pan for dinner this weekend. How much for *slow* class?"

"Parcel Post would be $6.60. But the trace costs twenty cents more."

"You charge more for a trace on second-class mail than for first class?"

"Yes. We have to make up for the lost postage somehow."

"All right, all ready… First Class. I've got the stamps, so don't print out one of those meter stamps."

"You've got that many stamps?"

In fact I did. You see, I'm a stamp collector, and when I order stamps from USPS Philatelic sales, they only sell them in quantities that are generally more than I need for my collection. So I've always got scads of extra stamps to use up. I was pulling stamps out of my surplus box, adding up values, to get the necessary $7.95.

"But you can't use those, Ed." She interrupted my counting, pointing to a particular strip of stamps I'd selected.

"Why not?"

"Those stamps are for bulk mail."

"Yeah… and this package is plenty bulky."

"And you can't use these either," she exclaimed. "They are for Non-Profit use."

"But they have a value, and I paid for them. They should be like legal tender. Why can't I use 'em toward the $7.95?"

"Because they were intended for other uses."

"Hey, these 24-centers were intended for post cards, yet I can use a bunch of *them*, can't I?"

"Ed, just give me your box of stamps and I'll figure it out for you."

She took the box of stamps and the package into the other room. When she returned, the stamps were affixed to the package. "There. All set to go," she proclaimed. "Here's your box of stamps back. I only used 4 cents more than the required postage."

"Four cents! You put an extra *four cents* on my package? How much more insurance will four cents buy?"

QUESTION OF THE DAY:

So, remind me, how do you get cooties?

Yes, I know, cooties are actually an informal reference to a rather serious malady. This Question of the Day is intended as a look back at my youthful recollections of its frivolous usage—long before I actually knew the implications. Such naivety has significantly lessened over the years, yet there is still a bit of fascination in returning to those halcyon, naïve days of long ago.

26

Back to When?

It seems the older I get, the more of my friends comment that they no longer wish to celebrate their birthday. It's almost as if they hope if they don't acknowledge the passage of another year, they can stay the same age. You gotta love optimists.

Reality aside, such comments of remaining at some idealistic age, do cause me some wonderment. At what age would I like to have remained?

One year old sounds good. I got just about everything that I wanted. At least I *think* I did. However, that's the problem with being one: you can't remember much. Somewhat like today... at least for me, anyway. So, I guess I don't need to be one again. I'm sure I've got everything I want; I just can't remember where I put it.

I can remember ten, though. Except for taking out the trash and doing dishes, I had no responsibilities. Gee, wouldn't that be a great era to languish in? Come to think of it, I'm not particularly responsible now, but I still take out the trash and help with dishes. So ten doesn't really hold much of an advantage over 65.

How about the teen years? There's definitely a tempting mystique about being a footloose and fancy-free youth. Yet, even those foolhardy years had drawbacks.

Girlfriends… or lack thereof, were a constant and often overwhelming challenge for me. And so was wrestling. No, not with the girls… as a sport.

Being small gave me a *chance* in that sport, but it wasn't necessarily an advantage. In all my other athletic endeavors, pint-sized stature was definitely a disadvantage. My body took a severe beating in most every sport I tried. Humph, my body takes a beating in about every game of softball I play today, so why be a teen?

Oh, for the glory years of post-teen. Twenty would surely be the age. Independence at last! Free to do as I please, when I please! So why, as my teen life waned, did I choose to attend college with its restrictive scheduling, required attendance, obligatory studying, and incessant testing? Not to mention the hectic pace. Why would I want to trade the leisure of retirement for that constraining regimen? Besides, even at my age I can still have an "all-nighter". Of course, in my college days, it was staying up all night. Now, it's *not getting up* during the night.

As I contemplate my past, it realize it was certainly filled with wondrous moments; yet I'm not so certain I want to repeat any year of my life. I suppose that's what is meant by the "Myth of Nostalgia". Our wistful thoughts of our past are often filled with grandeur. Nevertheless, with magnified reflection, our lives *back in the day* were not without drawbacks. I think I shall happily remain 65… or whatever age I am fortunate enough to achieve. At least I get senior discounts that were not available before.

QUESTION OF THE DAY:

Why does fat chance and slim chance mean the same thing?

Neither fat nor slim chance are applicable when figuring the odds that I will falter when interacting with modern electronics. I have an 8-track mind in a Blu-ray world. My computer literacy all but ceased when the C prompt went out the window. The GPS gal and I rarely get along well. Cell phones, I-pads, and scanners are perplexing… especially self check-out scanners.

27

Attendant Has Been Notified

Infrared scanners usually are installed at retail stores to cut down on the number of check-out clerks. I suspect they are also intended to speed up the process, as well, especially for those who only have a few things to purchase.

Though some assert that many customers have failed to master either simple mathematics or recognition of posted regulations, I shan't jump on a soap box. First of all, the soap boxes we purchase would not support a person of my physical stature, and second, my stature within this community is not sufficiently credible for anyone to pay much attention.

However, I *will* comment on the *sometimes senseless* sensitivity of the electronic *check-out clerk substitutes* commonly referred to as *self-scanners*—though that particular nomenclature eludes my logic. I have yet to discover a bar code on my *self*. Thus, I will refer to the machines as U-Scan.

Almost all retail check-outs include scanners. Human clerks sliding bar codes over magical red eyes are <u>not</u> double-checked by post-scan monitors or weight sensors. However, all *inhuman* U-Scan devices <u>are</u> double-checked. The persnickety functionality of these weight-sensing devices can make even the legitimate "less than 20 items" customer wonder just how this system's methodology expedites the check-out process. I am frequently mystified when a U-Scan voice proclaims, *"Attendant has been notified."*

For example: We make it a practice to take our own bags into the store. This requires an on-screen selection of "Use My Own Bag" as the first item of business in checking out at a U-Scan. Ah, but if you put your bag into the 'bagging' area prior to the computer advising you to do so... *Attendant has been notified* is audibly declared and checking-out suspended.

Snatching the ill-timed bag back does not rectify the situation; it only puts the computer into mode 2... *Unexpected item in the bagging area.* Whoa! What's that all about? I just removed the "unexpected item". What could it be? Residual dust that fell from the bag? Oh, wait, now I see the cause: Sue's coat is still in contact with one of the prongs of the bagging framework.

If you start checking out and then try to 'sneak' your own bag in along with 10 pounds of potatoes... *Attendant has been notified.* Seriously? 10 pounds, 2 ounces, and I'm under suspicion of thievery? I now understand why U-scans are not installed immediately opposite the exit doors. A strong gust of wind coming in the OUT door would summon an *Attendant* to every check-out station.

This electronic double-check for a couple of ounces of weight disparity is hardly consistent. If you put one 2-ounce package in the bagging area and then scan a second, identical item... *Attendant has been notified*. How can the 'system' validate the scaled weight of a single 2-ounce packet, yet cannot add 2 and 2 together?

Even more perplexing; If you have several such 2-ounce pouches, plus a hearing impairment, the ultimate U-scan meltdown is imminent. I have such an impairment. My hearing aids are marvelous instruments of sound enhancement, yet they often can't communicate with my brain as to the direction from which the synthesized sound comes. Directionality is remarkably obscure in noisy environments. Noise, especially groans of other frustrated U-Scanners mingled with incessant beeping of multiple scanners, is endemic in check-out lanes. So, I often cannot tell which scanner is beeping.

Consequently, as Sue scans a single packet of white chili mix and I proceed to drop each of five more identical packets into our bag, coincident to the beep of her scan, I confuse a beep from the adjacent U-scan as one from ours, and *Unexpected item...*

The main problem is that the device won't accept a make-up scan. Nor would it tolerate my attempt to remove the, presumably, offending packet. Compound that with the inadvertent relocation of one of the cloth straps of our bag to rest on the U-scan console... *Attendant has been notified*.

My attempt to correct the ill-timed drop of the chili packet put the U-Scan computer into a "double-crossed" algorithm which disabled any meaningful interaction—though I must admit, I have been known to illogically mutter my categorically immoral thoughts to this inhuman object of my dismay. Also illogically, I have uttered apologetic contrition for foolishly allowing my bag strap to wander off, or Sue's coat to touch the scanner's sensitive areas. Logically, however, absolution is never granted… because… *Attendant has been notified*—and remission of these sins is not an option.

Like a thief in total surrender, I throw the chili packets down and my hands up, awaiting the check-out officer. Periodically, our scanner's voice reiterates, *Attendant has been notified.* When the *Attendant* does finally arrive, but has not yet interceded on our behalf, the scanner once again repeats itself. I quickly leaned between the *Attendant* and the scan screen. "Be patient… she's here now. It will all be over soon."

The *Attendant* looked at me quizzically… or perhaps it was that look of certain understanding why I had had so much trouble checking out. She quickly punched a bunch of numbers on her hand-held device. As I watched the combination of key-punches, I imagined she was dialing a phone number. I fully expected her device to announce *Attendant has been notified*—quite possibly an *attendant* wearing a white coat and carrying a funny-looking, very long-armed jacket.

QUESTION OF THE DAY:

If you were to offer me a penny for my thoughts, and I give you my two cents worth, do I get change?

I do not understand why so many people consider unsolicited phone calls as an infringement on their privacy. I am not aware of any regulation which requires anyone to reveal any personal information, let alone answer questions truthfully.

28

Survey Says...

I've disliked election time since one of the National Conventions preempted Howdy Doody. It's not that I don't value my voting right, nor do I necessarily want to ignore information about candidates, though I do wonder about the validity of much of the hype every 4 years.

I'm just irritated at the onslaught of hollow rhetoric, unsubstantiated innuendos, and outright disparaging remarks.

My other irritation associated with elections is excessive ringing in my ears. And I'm not talking tinnitus—I'm referring to the phone. "Do Not Call" membership does not exclude political auto-dialers. Fortunately, *Caller ID* helps me decide whether to answer or not. The other night, I was not particularly busy and decided to answer "Ogden UT". In my very best 90-year-old voice—and mentality—I answered.

A decidedly young female asked if I had a few minutes to answer a short survey. With a mix of geriatrics and theatrics, I replied: "My dear, at this point in my life, time is about all I do have. Plus, my doctor says answerin' questions is a good way to keep my mind sharp. I hope to get them correct."

"Sir, there are no correct answers to these questions. We are asking for your opinion."

"Well, that's good to know. I'm feeling much more comfortable now."

"First I must tell you that this call may be monitored or recorded. Please verify your name."

I waited a few seconds. "Go ahead, I'm ready. Will this be a multiple-choice question?"

"Actually, I need *you* to tell me your name."

"You mean you called *me* and don't know my name?"

"That is correct. You have been randomly selected to participate in this survey, so I don't actually know your name. Would you share that with me, please?"

"Sam… Uncle Sam. That's what they call me here at the home, 'cause there are two Sams livin' here and he's young enough to be my nephew."

She thanked me and proceeded with the survey. After a few questions to which I gave somewhat thoughtful answers, she said she was going to ask my opinion on the Proposals.

I'm not sure why she started at the bottom, but she continued: "Are you familiar with Proposal 6?"

"Six, huh? I read 'em all but I cain't say as I know 'em by number."

"Only to refresh your memory, Proposal 6 is to amend the Constitution regarding the construction of bridges and tunnels. If you were to vote today, would you vote yes or no?"

"I voted last week. I wouldn't want to cancel that and vote again today."

"I'm sorry, I didn't mean that you'd actually be voting today. I'm only asking how you *might* vote if the election was today."

"Well, my dear, I would not change my mind from what I thought last week."

We went around in circles for a minute or so on whether she could reword the questions so as to not confuse me and/or not violate my right to privacy on how I voted. Finally we agreed that it was okay for me to pretend that I had not yet voted. That was good, especially considering that I was already pretending.

She went on; "Proposal 6 is to amend the Constitution regarding..."

"Oh... No. I'd vote against anything to change the Constitution. I think we have a good Constitution. It don't need changin'."

"Then you would vote 'No' on Proposal 6."

"I voted 'No' on all the proposals to change the Constitution."

"Thank you. I'll check 'No' for Proposal 6. The next proposal I'm going to ask you about is number 5. Only to refresh your memory, Proposal 5 is to amend the Constitution to limit the enactment..."

"There you go again, trying to change the Constitution. Don't you think we have a good Constitution already?"

"I'm sorry sir, I'm not allowed to give my opinion during the survey."

"Well, I'm interested in your opinion as much as you are mine. If I call you back will you tell me what you think?"

"I'm sorry sir, there is no call-back number."

"Well, then, can you call me after you get off work?"

"I don't have your phone number. This call originated by dialing your number at random."

"No problem. It's 876-555-4321. But you'll have to ask for Uncle Sam, 'cause you never know who'll be answering the phone around here."

Needless to say, she declined to call me back. During the next half-hour of repartee, she never really laughed at any of my responses. That would have been rude, but only if I actually was a dim-witted, cantankerous, old man. However, I did notice that her amusement throughout the call and good wishes to me at the close of the call did not seem scripted.

QUESTION OF THE DAY:

On TV, the commercial says that 8 out of 10 people suffer from hemorrhoids. Does this mean the other 2 people enjoy them?

I suppose most people do not perceive inferences like I do from indeterminate commercial statements as mentioned above. I also suppose most people perceive my mental acuity to wobble off center.

29

Sleep, Off-Center

I have apnea and use a CPAP; that's an acronym for a machine that blows my nose… inward.

In my judgment, the machine hasn't been doing an adequate job lately. It's functioning correctly, but the pressure settings didn't seem to be adequate. So, I needed to be retested.

My doctor scheduled the sleep study at a Sleep Center in Lansing. He gave me a brochure. Wow! This sounded like an overnight stay at a resort, compared to the similar study I had done at a hospital. Well, my study was last night.

As I entered the Sleep Center at my appointed time, a young lady greeted me. "Good evening. You must be Mr. Kaiser."

"*Mister?* Kaiser. No, *Mister* Kaiser would be my father. I'm Ed."

"Oh…" she said, looking past me into the entry, "then is he right behind you?"

"I don't think so. We buried him several years ago."

"Oh, my, I'm so very sorry. I..." The other young lady in the office interrupted: "Relax a little, Nicole. Hi, Ed. I'm Heather. I spoke with you on the phone yesterday. Be alert to his chicanery, Nicole, but I think you'll enjoy being his tech tonight."

Okay, so maybe my pre-procedure interview with Heather wasn't exactly cut and dried. She had many boring questions, and I didn't want to be boring. After we got through all the insurance and vital statistics, she inquired why I needed retesting. She rapid-fired a bunch of questions like: Has your snoring increased? Are you restless during the night? Do you wake up tired?

She inquired, "Do you wake up with headaches that require medication to alleviate?"

I answered, "I must admit that, occasionally, Sue says I AM the headache."

"Do you feel depressed, or are you taking anything to combat depression?"

"Aaaah... you mean, like, toss down a Red, to get high now and then?"

"Prescription drugs, is what I mean."

"No."

"Do you think your CPAP is too high?"

"Nope. I never give my CPAP any uppers."

She laughed, "Never, mind. Do you take naps?"

"No."

"Do you ever fall asleep during the day?"

"Nnngggggghhhh," I mimicked a loud snore.

She laughed again, and my reputation was implanted in her mind.

That was yesterday. Last night was Nicole's turn. As she led me to my room, I commented on how impressive their brochure was. "I'm really looking forward to breakfast."

"I'm sorry, sir, we don't serve breakfast."

"But, look," I said, showing her the brochure. "It has breakfast listed under Patient Services."

"Well, you see, that's not our brochure. It's our company's. They've got lots of locations around Michigan, but we don't have all of that stuff."

Looking at the first item on the list of amenities, I inquired; "Do I get a Queen size, pillow-top mattress?"

"I don't know about 'pillow-top', but it's comfortable."

Entering the room, I noticed there was no bathroom, and I pointed to that item on the list. "So, I see I don't have a private bathroom, with shower, either."

"It's across the hall. You can lock it. That's as private as you can get."

"Says here you provide towels, toiletries and hairdryer with the private shower? Is that an error too?"

"No, the shower is down the hall. You can lock that room, too, so it qualifies as private. I'll get you fresh towels in the morning. You probably won't need a hairdryer."

Hmmm, I probably deserved that, considering my baldness is more comparable to a vulture than an eagle.

"Well, that will be fine. I'm really glad for the locks. I guess that will have to be private enough. And speaking of privacy, are those *cameras* in the corners of the room?"

"Yes, we need to monitor your overnight activity."

"I don't expect an abundance of activity once you get all those wires hooked up to me."

"Yes, we do have a lot to hook you up to. Please take off your shirt and have a seat."

In consideration of her diminutive stature, I offered to squat on the floor while she hooked up the EEG monitors on top of my head. I'm not certain: possibly she lost her balance and slipped while retrieving the bundle of wires from the cart over my shoulder; or, maybe it was a well-disguised "accident". Either way, I probably deserved the lashing. Anyway, she retrieved her tube of glue from the cart and proceeded to stick wires everywhere.

They wired me for EEG, EKG, TMJ, REM, PLM, SOL, and a few other letters I can't remember. They even monitored my eyeballs.

With all those wires, plus my CPAP hose pony-tailed off of my skull, I was wondering how I'd ever get comfortable.

But somehow, I did, and I ended up having a fairly good night's rest. In the morning, as promised, I had fresh, very plush, towels with my shower, and Nicole gave me a mint patty in lieu of breakfast. Remarkably thoughtful considering all the trouble I gave her the night before.

QUESTION OF THE DAY:

If there's no time like the present, why wait to present a present?

Presents are present most notably each December. At least for our family they are. Also at that time of year, in addition to the presents is the presence of Christmas decorations.

30

Hanging of the Greens

Hanging of the Greens! The ritual of converting the home from the blahs of winter to the exciting décor of the holidays. It's almost magical how Sue transforms mundane to magnificent, especially at Christmas. And every year she comes up with new ways to decorate… new realms of wonderland to venture into… surprises in decorating that never cease to amaze me. Mind you, these are not whims birthed in late November. Some of her plans are conceived months earlier.

If she'd just talk about some of her ideas as they develop, I might be a little more prepared. But no, she fosters these ideas alone, eventually delivering them with a simple, "Ed, I've been thinking…" By that time, it's too late to abort. The brainchild is born, unfortunately with traces of mutation.

A good example: her bathroom decorations. Decorate the living room? Certainly a good idea. Bathroom? That's a functional room. You go there for one purpose and it's not to enjoy yuletide motif. It is nice to sit in the living room with friends and chat in the ambiance of warm candlelight flickering amongst greenery, garlands and glass balls.

But, can you imagine the reaction when guests come to visit and you say, "Since my wife's done such a splendid job of decorating the bathroom, I thought maybe we'd relax on the edge of the tub this evening."

I'm not opposed to candles in the bathroom. We use them in there all year long, so putting a ring of pine sprigs and cones with some ribbon seemed appropriate enough. I guess I didn't even object to the (scaled down) antique sled, either. I thought it was a clever place to put the wash cloth and soap, but that thought paved the way for a collision of visions. My eyes see function, while Sue's vision is ethereal. Our divergent views are bound to collide.

After working in the basement the other night, I washed up for dinner. Sue happened to go into the bathroom later in the evening. She quickly emerged.

"Who used the soap in the sleigh?" (Like someone else but me might have been the culprit.)

"Why?" I responded. (Really a dumb question, considering the tone of her voice.)

"You're not supposed to *use* it. It's just *decoration*."

"It's soap, right? Just because it has red and white stripes and smells like a candy cane shouldn't deter my using it to wash my hands."

"They aren't stripes, they're swishes of pigment infused in clear resin."

"Resin? It's not *soap*?"

"I put that away until after Christmas. It wasn't very festive-looking."

"So, when I want to wash, I need to dig the soap out of a drawer? I don't suppose I should've used the wash cloth in the sled either?"

"You *didn't!*"

"Well, yaaah. But I hung it up on the towel ring to dry."

"Ed, you should have gotten a hint not to use them because they were in a sleigh with pretty Christmas ornaments."

"Now that you mention it, those glass balls made it tough to get to the wash cloth. This probably isn't a good time to complain about the soap, is it?"

"What, you don't think the soap is pretty?"

"Oh, it's pretty, all right. It's just not a very good soap. When I dried my hands on the towel I left some streaks."

"*Please*, don't tell me you used the white towel draped through the antique brass horn."

"Don't worry, dear, I re-tied the ribbon and stuck the poinsettias back in the folds."

So, you see, she had a vision of grandeur even for the commonplace amenities of the bathroom. I just need closer supervision so that I don't hang *myself* in the greens.

*To order additional copies of this book
and to see other books published by Buttonwood Press
visit us online at www.buttonwoodpress.com*